Vera B. Williams

IT'S A GINGERBREAD HOUSE

Bake It, Build It, Eat It!

A MULBERRY PAPERBACK BOOK
New York

The Library of Congress has cataloged the Greenwillow Books edition of
It's a Gingerbread House as follows:
Williams, Vera B. It's a gingerbread house (Greenwillow read-alone
books) Summary: Simple instructions for baking and constructing a
gingerbread house.
1. Gingerbread house—Juvenile literature.
[1. Gingerbread houses. 2. Cake. 3. Christmas cookery]
I. Title. TX739.W53 641.8'654 77-25979

10 9 8 7 6 5 4 3 2 1
First Mulberry Edition, 1996
ISBN 0-688-14980-4

For Sarah, Jenny,

and Merce,

with whom I first

made these houses

CONTENTS

FROM
GRANDPA BEN
#6 778 GILFORD ST.
VANCOUVER, B.C.
CANADA
Y6G 2N4

FRAGILE

TO
CARRIE, BENNY, SAM
WILLOW GROVE RD.
STONY PT. N.Y. 10980
U.S.A.

A week before Christmas

a box came to the house.

On Christmas Eve the children opened it.

It was a gingerbread house

their grandpa had baked for them.

It had a door and windows.

It was trimmed with frosting

and nuts and candies.

"It is like a house in a fairy tale," Benny said.

"It smells like cookies," Carrie said.

"I want to eat it."

"We can't eat it," Sam said,

"until everyone sees it at Christmas."

"Not even a little taste?" Carrie asked.

Benny and Sam gave in.

They broke off a bit of the roof.

At bedtime they took a last look

at the gingerbread house.

Benny said, "Wasn't there a little cat

by that door?"

Their mother laughed and said,

"Nibble, nibble, mousekin,

Who's nibbling on our housekin?"

But no one answered.

On Christmas Day Benny and Sam
stood guard over the gingerbread house.
"No more nibbles," they said.
"The little cat is already missing.
The roof has a big bite out of it.
The six red cinnamon hearts are gone.
We want to keep the rest."
But Carrie said, "Come on!
We can at least eat the jelly beans.
And the nuts.
And the gumdrops.
And the frosting.
And the shutters.
And the door."

When they finished,

the house looked very plain.

Benny said,

"I wish we knew how to make another one.

Then I wouldn't mind eating all of this."

"Oh, let's eat it anyway," Carrie said.

"If we tell Grandpa how much we liked it,

he'll make us another one next year."

So they ate the roof.

Then they saw there was a little chest
made of gingerbread inside the house.
They took the lid off the chest.
There was a letter inside.

Dear Carrie, Benny, and Sam,

I guess by now
you have eaten the roof.
Eat the whole house.
Then you can make another one.
I've written down everything
you need to know to make it.

Read the recipe
and the directions
and see where you will need help.
Ask a grownup who likes to bake
to help you.

It takes about six hours.
But you don't make it all in one day.
You cut out the cardboard pattern
and mix the dough one time.

Later on you roll the dough
and cut out and bake
the walls and roof.

Let the pieces dry overnight.
Then you make the frosting
and use it
to stick the house together
and to decorate it.

I made a list of what you need
for each thing you do.
Read the lists and
make your own shopping list.

GOOD LUCK AND LOVE,

Grandpa Ben

P.S. Please don't worry
if your house doesn't look
exactly like the pictures.
I'm sure if you do your best
to follow the directions
your house will turn out great.

G.B.

THE PATTERN

To make the four pattern pieces

you need:

- carbon paper, pencil, scissors
- paper you can see through

  for tracing
- and cardboard you can cut easily

Read the directions on

the patterns on pages 46 and 47.

Place the carbon paper

shiny side down

under the patterns

on pages 46 and 47.

Place the cardboard

under the carbon.

Put the paper over the pattern

so you don't draw right in the book.

Now trace with a pencil.

Check that the drawing
is going through
onto the cardboard.

Cut out each cardboard pattern
carefully.

You will have
four cardboard patterns.
Your house will fit together better
if your patterns are exact.

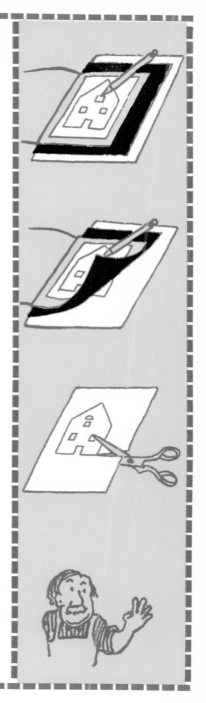

THE DOUGH

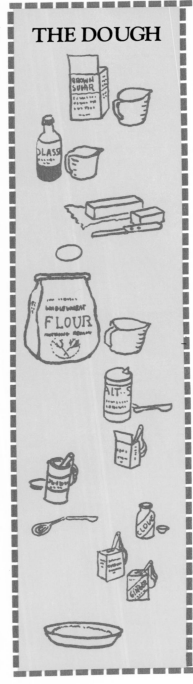

To make the dough you need:

- ¾ cup of dark brown sugar

- ¾ cup of dark molasses

- 1½ sticks of butter or margarine

- 1 egg

- 4½ cups of wholewheat flour

- 1 teaspoon salt

- ½ teaspoon baking soda

- 1 teaspoon baking powder

- ¼ teaspoon cloves

- 1 teaspoon cinnamon

- 1 tablespoon ginger

- some white flour to keep the dough from sticking

- a big bowl

- a wooden mixing spoon

- a rubber scraper

- a small strainer

- a measuring cup

- measuring spoons

- a medium-sized pot

- waxed paper

First you make the molasses part.

Then you mix the flour part.

Then you put them together
and form the dough
into a smooth lump.

THE MOLASSES PART

Put the molasses in the pot.

Put the brown sugar in the pot.

Cut up the butter or margarine

and put it in the pot.

Heat all this until it bubbles a little.

Take it off the stove.

Wait until it is lukewarm.
Add the egg and
mix until it disappears.

20

Measure the wholewheat flour
right into the big bowl.

Don't press the flour
or shake it down
in the cup or you will
have too much.

Put the baking soda,
the baking powder,
the salt, the cinnamon,
the cloves, and the ginger
through the strainer into the flour
so there will be no hard lumps.

Now stir until the spices
are all mixed.
Then stir some more.
It is important to mix well here.

MIXING THE MOLASSES AND THE FLOUR

Make a place for a lake in the flour.

Pour in all the molasses mixture.

Mix it slowly at first,

then harder until it is all one color.

It will be very thick.

If you can't get it all mixed

with a spoon, use your hands.

Then scrape all the dough

off your fingers into the bowl

(except for a taste).

Now you are going to make

the dough into a smooth lump.

This is easy if nothing sticks.

So put away

the things you won't need.

Wipe off the work place.

Be sure your hands are clean and dry.

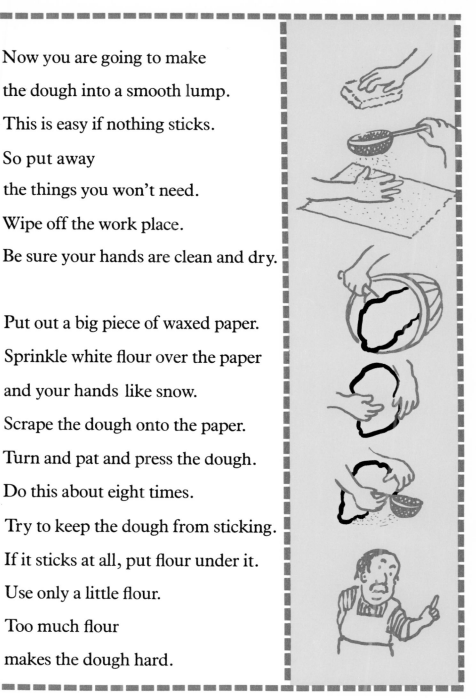

Put out a big piece of waxed paper.

Sprinkle white flour over the paper

and your hands like snow.

Scrape the dough onto the paper.

Turn and pat and press the dough.

Do this about eight times.

Try to keep the dough from sticking.

If it sticks at all, put flour under it.

Use only a little flour.

Too much flour

makes the dough hard.

When the dough is smooth like clay,
pat it into a shape
something like a book
and put it in a plastic bag.
Let the dough rest
while you do something else
for a few hours.

Don't put it in the refrigerator.
Cold dough is very hard to roll out.
If you have to wait a few days
to bake the dough,
you'll have to put it
in the refrigerator.
But be sure to take it out
at least three hours
before you need it.
Now you are ready to roll the dough
and to cut it out and to bake it.

ROLL, CUT, AND BAKE

ROLL

For rolling you need:

- a rolling pin

- two of your largest flat pans

- oil to grease pans

- a small sharp knife

- a pencil

- and white flour

First turn your pans

UPSIDE DOWN.

Be sure the backs are clean because

you are going to roll the dough

right on the backs of the pans.

You are going to cut out the pieces

right on the backs of the pans too.

1.
Rub oil on the backs
of the pans.

2.
Now make
a dough thickness tester.
Mark ⅛″ with a pencil
at the end of a knife.

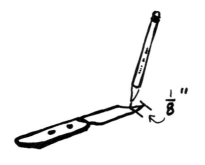

3.
Wash and dry your hands.
Put flour on your hands
and on the rolling pin.

4.
Pat out half the dough
like this.

5.

Then roll it out this thin all over. You don't need to press really hard. You will see the dough spread out.

6.

If someone holds the pan steady, you can keep rolling firmly and evenly.

7.

If the rolling pin sticks, flour it.
Keep checking thickness with the tester.

8.

Try to get the dough to cover the pan. Don't worry if the edges get too thin. You don't use them.

CUT

For cutting you need:

- a small pointed knife
- some white flour
- and your patterns

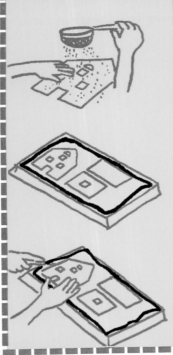

Ask a grownup
to set the oven at 375.
Sprinkle a little flour
on each pattern.
Lay the patterns
on the dough.
Hold the pattern steady
and cut close.
Cut all the way through the dough.

Peel off the extra dough
and save it.

Put it in a plastic bag
so it doesn't get dry.

Cut out the door and windows,
and save the pieces.

Make shutters from
the window pieces.
Don't forget to bake these too.

Make a few extra cookies.
You will need them
to taste and to test.

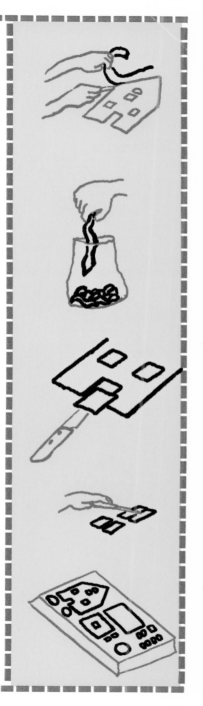

BAKE

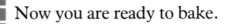
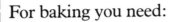

Now you are ready to bake.

For baking you need:

- a pancake turner
- and potholders

Bake both pans at the same time
if you can fit them in the oven
so they are close to the center.
You need help to decide
when the pieces are done.
After ten minutes they should be
much darker brown
than the unbaked dough
and have a good strong spicy smell.
After you take them out of the oven,
try a test cookie
when you can hold it easily.

It *must* be crisp all the way through.
Cookies that are soft when cool
will not stand up.

If the test cookie is not crisp,
bake all the cookies some more.
Check often!
If some get too dark,
take out the dark ones
and let the rest bake.

After you take the pans out,
let the pans cool
until you can hold them.

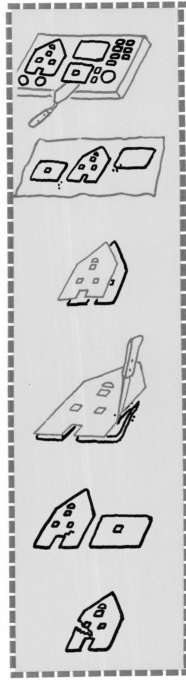

Then lift the pieces off
while they are still warm.
Loosen them all around if they stick.

Lay them on a flat place to cool.
Do not put them on racks.

While they are still warm,
check the size with your pattern
like this.

If a piece is too big or crooked,
trim it with a sharp knife. Be careful.
If a piece is a tiny bit too small
or has a little crack or a chip,
you can try to fix it
with the frosting later.

You can fix a lot with frosting.
But if the piece is really too small
or has a big crack, make a new one.

You should have two end walls,

two side walls, two roof pieces,

doors, and shutters.

If you need to bake more pieces,

rub all the crumbs off the pan.

Oil the pan again and

do everything

just as you did before.

If you want any little animals,

people, or a truck,

make them now.

Save the patterns and enough dough

for another wall in case

you break one.

Now you can turn off the oven.

The cookies must dry out overnight,

so put them in a safe place

where they are not piled up

or covered.

Don't make the frosting

until you are ready

to put the house together.

Once you start the frosting

you must go on to finish your house.

The frosting gets hard if you leave it.

To make the frosting you need:

- the whites of 2 eggs
- 3 cups of powdered sugar
- ½ teaspoon cream of tartar
- 2 tablespoons lemon juice
- 2 medium-sized bowls
- a flour sifter or strainer
- a spoon

THE FROSTING

First you have to separate the whites from the yolks of the eggs. You might need help with this. Save the yolks to add to scrambled eggs. Put the sifter over a medium-sized bowl. Put the powdered sugar and cream of tartar through the sifter to get out the lumps.

Take a spoon and mix the sugar
into the egg whites a little at a time
until you use up 2½ cups of sugar.
Don't worry if the mixture
is lumpy at first.
Add the lemon juice
to the sugar mixture.
Mix and mix.
It should be as thick and smooth
as soft ice cream or mashed potatoes.

If it is not thick enough,
add more sugar.
If it is too thick,
add more lemon juice.

Cover the bowl with plastic wrap.
Now you are ready
to build and decorate.

You need a base for your house.

A breadboard, a low box,

or a baking pan covered with

aluminum foil makes a good base.

You will also need the frosting,

a knife to spread it with,

and a toothpick

to frost the smaller places.

Use candies, nuts, dried fruits,

and candied fruits for decorations.

Pick ones that look good

as well as taste good.

Read the whole next part

before you start to build.

BUILD AND DECORATE

1.
Lay your floor pattern

on the base.

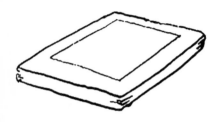

2.
Brush all the crumbs

off your pieces.

3.
Take the front wall.

4.
Spread frosting this thick

5.

and to cover well

here

and here.

6.

Stand the front wall

in its place

Don't stand it

right on the pattern.

Hold it there firmly.

7.

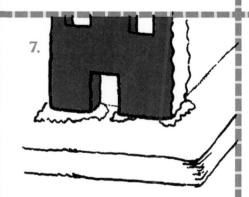

Don't worry if frosting

squeezes out and shows.

8.
Take a side wall.

Spread frosting along here.

9. Put the side wall in place. Check that it stands right along the edge of the floor pattern.

10. Have one person hold it so the walls stick together at the base and the side.

11. Take the back wall.

12.

Spread frosting here

and here.

13.
Press the back wall
into place. Check it with
the floor pattern.

Hold all three walls together
until the frosting gets firm.

14.
After five minutes
take your hands away.

If the walls don't stick,
hold them longer. Ten
minutes should be plenty.

15.
Take the other side wall.

16.
Frost along

here,

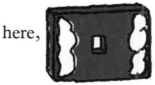

here,

and here.

17.

Put this side wall in place.

If the first three walls fit,

the fourth wall will fit.

18.

You might have to jiggle it

a little or put in more

frosting   for a good fit.

19.

Hold until the frosting sets.

Don't put on the roof until

your house will stand alone.

20.

Spread frosting all along

here.

The roof pieces are bigger.

They hang over the walls

all around.

21.

Take both roof pieces.

Frost along here.

Frost along here.

22.

Put them in place

with the frosted edges

joined as close as possible

along the top.

23.

Hold the roof

until it stays by itself.

There will be a crack here.

Don't worry. You can fill it

with decorations.

24.

Put the shutters

and the doors in place.

Now you are ready

to decorate.

43

Here are some ideas you can try.

Cut slices from gumdrops.

Press them into the windows

for colored glass.

Use the slices around the doors

and windows for designs.

Use bits of peanut brittle

and sesame squares to edge the walls.

Use halves of almonds and walnuts

to edge the roof.

Use nuts and candies that fit into

the roof crack to decorate the top.

Pile up candies for a chimney.

Try thin round candies for shingles

or try pumpkin seeds or flat cookies.

Have a good time

finishing your house.

Have a good time
showing it
to everyone.

And have
a good time
eating it.

(Give the crumbs
to the birds for a treat.)

THE BLACK OUTLINE ON THIS PAGE IS A FLOOR PATTERN
YOU WILL USE AS A GUIDE TO PUT THE HOUSE TOGETHER.
DO NOT MAKE A COOKIE FROM THIS PATTERN.

THE RED OUTLINE ON THIS PAGE IS THE PATTERN
FOR BOTH SIDES OF THE ROOF. USE IT TWICE.

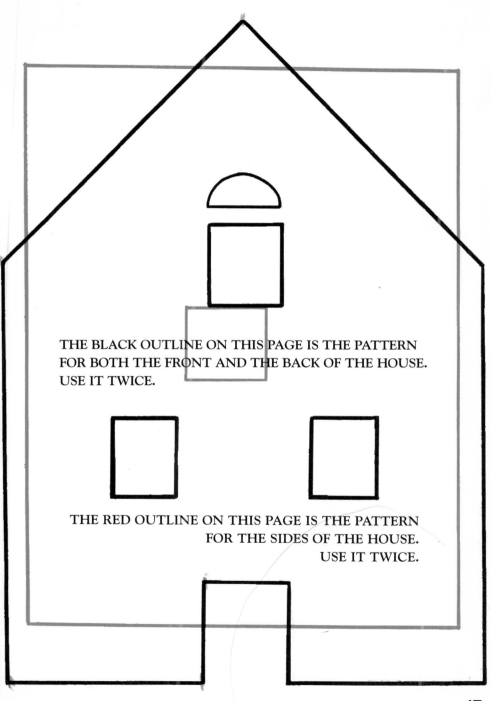

THE BLACK OUTLINE ON THIS PAGE IS THE PATTERN
FOR BOTH THE FRONT AND THE BACK OF THE HOUSE.
USE IT TWICE.

THE RED OUTLINE ON THIS PAGE IS THE PATTERN
FOR THE SIDES OF THE HOUSE.
USE IT TWICE.

685